Ricky Roogle

Impostor
Notebook

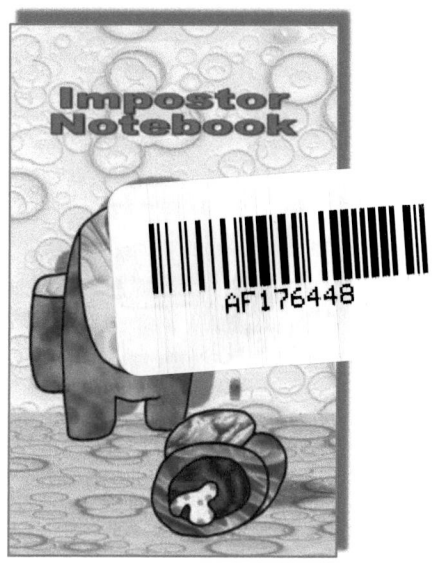

NOT AN OFFICIAL INNERSLOTH PRODUCT. NOT APPROVED BY OR ASSOCIATED WITH INNERSLOTH.

Bibliografische Information der Deutschen Nationalbibliothek:
Die Deutsche Nationalbibliothek verzeichnet diese Publikation in der
Deutschen Nationalbibliografie; detaillierte bibliografische
Daten sind im Internet über http://dnb.dnb.de abrufbar.

© 2021 Ricky Roogle; 1. Auflage
Covergraphic, text & illustrations © 2021 Ricky Roogle
contact author: ricky.roogle@t-online.de
Herstellung und Verlag: BoD – Books on Demand, Norderstedt
ISBN: 9783752658200

SUPER COLORING BOOK for Ameng.us Fans

CREWMATES COLORING BOOK for Ameng.us Fans

The SUPER MAZE BOOK for Ameng.us Fans

PASSWORD LOGBOOK for Ameng.us Fans

MATH COLORING BOOK for Ameng.us Fans

HOW TO DRAW SKINS for Ameng.us Fans

WORD SEARCH PUZZLES for Ameng.us Fans

SUPER QUIZ BOOK for Ameng.us Fans

CARTOONS MEMES and JOKES for Ameng.us Fans

WTF!

Notebook

Crewmate Notebook

Impostor Notebook